STEAM MEMORIES 1950

No.4: North Eastern Lines:
York, Newcastle, Darlington, Hull, Alnmouth, Starbeck, and more...

Book Law Publications

Copyright Book Law Publications 2007
ISBN 978-1901-945-829

INTRODUCTION

The photographer Don Beecroft started building up his portfolio of railway photographs during the mid-1950's, at a time of great transition on British Railways. Like many of his generation he had a great fondness for the steam locomotive but that fondness did not, at first, embrace the new diesel locomotives which were then being introduced. Although he did take the occasional photograph of diesel units, he concentrated, like many of us, on the dwindling stocks of steam. We all knew, in the pits of our stomachs, that steam was on its way out and diesel traction, in its various forms, was here to stay. Don Beecroft went on a mission to capture as many images of the steam locomotive as he could, wherever he could, time and monetary budgets permitting - he still had to earn a living in post-war Britain.

This album represent some of the images he recorded on what was then the BR North Eastern Region but what was essentially former North Eastern Railway territory. Presented alphabetically, the images illustrate trains, locomotives and locations between Alnmouth in the north, Neville Hill in the south, Hull (and others) on the coast, with lots of places in-between. Hopefully the feel of the working railway of the period will reflect in these pictures - there are many more to come in a series of illustrated books showing off the British Railways of memory.

(title page) **Just to the south of North Seaton station Don Beecroft caught this mineral train on film in September 1966. J27 No.65838 was the motive power and looking at the wisps of steam it has everything nicely in check.** *BLP - DB8317.*

Printed and bound by The Amadeus Press, Cleckheaton, West Yorkshire.
First published in the United Kingdom by Book Law Publications, 382 Carlton Hill, Nottingham, NG4 1JA.

In May 1964 Alnmouth could still offer a reasonable selection of motive power passing through, working the various branches or resting on the shed. Here Peppercorn K1 No.62021 rests on the coaling road whilst other K1's allocated to this sub shed on this date were out working and included No.62011 which was hauling a goods train on the Amble branch, and No.62025 on the Alnwick branch. The engine shed at Alnmouth dated from 1875 though the station was opened much earlier. Up to 1892 both station and engine shed were known as Bilton Junction. Up to their demise in 1957, Alnmouth shed could boast to housing the last six D20 4-4-0 tender engines still working on BR, a fine pedigree indeed. However, by the end of 1962 the reliable Peppercorn 'moguls' had taken over the shed workings with No.62021 arriving from Gateshead on 25th November 1962. No.62025 had been transferred from Heaton some three weeks previously with No.62006 and 62023. No.62011, along with No.62012, transferred from Fort William shed in early December. All six worked at Alnmouth until closure of the engine shed on 19th June 1966 after which the six K1's parted company and went to various sheds on Tyneside and Wearside. Another K1 arrived from Gateshead in November 1962, No.62030, but this one departed in February 1965 forSunderland and less than six months later it was condemned and sold for scrap. Virtually taking its place, if slightly prematurely, was No.62050 which had come from Consett shed. This 2-6-0 hung around to the end and was sent away with the rest at closure. *BLP - DB6733* 3

Later that morning a York based Peppercorn A1, No.60121 SILURIAN, arrived at Alnmouth station with a special from Newcastle to Edinburgh. A small number of main line expresses stopped at this place then (and still do today), so this special was nothing out of the ordinary. Shortly after the 1964 Summer Working Timetable was completed, the Pacific was withdrawn and in November it was sold for scrap. The shed's by now shelterless coal bank can be seen on the right of the picture. *BLP - DB6735.*

Another northbound working thundered through Alnmouth that morning in the shape of V2 No.60812 on a Down coal train. This was a Gateshead engine and was probably hauling fuel to Tweedmouth shed which still had a sizeable allocation in 1964. Based on Tyneside for the whole of its twenty-seven year life, at either Heaton or Gateshead, No.60812 was condemned just a few weeks after this scene was committed to film. For some strange reason, which has never been explained properly to the writer, a number of V2's were sent to Swindon Works for scrapping in October 1964 and this particular engine was amongst their number - an inappropriate end to an otherwise exemplary career. Note the engine shed on the right; during 1887 the two-road building was doubled in length to accommodate the extra engines required for working the new branch opened between Alnwick and Coldstream. *BLP - DB6740.*

V2 No.60982 calls at Alnmouth with the 7.30 a.m. Berwick-Newcastle stopping train in May 1964. On the Down side island platform K1 No.62025, working the Alnwick branch train, hides behind the signal. The station here opened for business in October 1850. In 1887 a larger station was fashioned from the old one and the original buildings were incorporated into the new accommodation on the Up side. Today the island platform is simply the Down platform with a waiting shelter having replaced the canopied buildings seen here. The Up side building have all be demolished and a new brick building with a pitched roof and containing the necessary passenger facilities has taken its place. What of the V2? Well this one had a more dignified exit compared with No.60812. A York engine at the time of this photograph (and had been for its twenty years except for a few weeks in 1953 and again in 1955 when it was loaned to Darlington), it was withdrawn just three months later and entered Darlington Works for cutting up on Friday 16th October 1964. *BLP - DB6741.*

A visit to Bridlington engine shed on any summer weekend from 1959 to 1965 would make anyone believe that the depot was fully functional. However, things were not always as they appeared in some quarters of British Railways and Bridlington shed was one of them. Closed officially on 1st December 1958, the depot was left intact to function as a stabling point for visiting locomotives during the summer seasons thereafter. Its last locomotive allocation consisted of two Class G5 0-4-4 tank engines which transferred away on 8th June to Dairycoates shed. The last decent sized motive power to leave the place were five D49 'Shires' which reallocated in September 1957. So, to see a tender engine stabled on the shed after the summer of 1957 meant that it was a foreigner as is B16 No.61471 (61402 until 15th December 1949) seen stabled in the yard in June 1960. The Neville Hill 4-6-0 had brought in a train from Leeds and is turned ready to work back home. K3 No.61932 of Dairycoates, standing behind on one of the shed roads, has brought in an excursion from Hull. *BLP* - 7 *DB3622.*

Another Neville Hill B16, No.61411, rests inside Bridlington shed in June 1960. Considering the shed had been 'abandoned' for nearly two years its condition is remarkably clean and tidy. This building was the third engine shed to carry the title Bridlington and it opened in 1893, replacing a two-road York & North Midland Railway shed dating from 1875 and which stood virtually where this picture was taken. Note the typical North Eastern Railway fluted smoke vents which required engines to be positioned accurately on the shed roads rather than just being stabled. The sole occupant would soon be sharing the shed with new arrivals from virtually anytown situated in the Midlands or through the north of England to the Borders. No.61411 would transfer to Mirfield shed during the following October but its stay there would be short because in September 1961 it was condemned and afterwards cut up at Darlington Works. Note that the clock reads 0810 hours or has it stopped as the time is more likely to be noon or slightly later. *BLP - DB3624.*

From Ardsley shed in June 1960 we have B1 No.61039 STEINBOK which has brought an excursion into Bridlington from Wakefield. Note that the tender on the right, belonging to another B1 no doubt, has the wrong type of BR emblem; the lion should, of course, be facing in the opposite direction, to the left. Behind that tender is another Neville Hill B16, No.61412 - the populace of Leeds certainly enjoyed their day trips to Bridlington. This engine shed remained standing until 1986 when demolition was ordered. *BLP - DB3801.*

The ex WD 0-6-0ST purchased by the LNER were useful engines and could be found all over the former system. Darlington Locomotive Works utilised a number of them for shunting dead engines and materials around the workshops and yards. On a sunny Saturday afternoon in June 1957, Nos.68045 and 68008 languish in the main yard of the works just outside the Erecting Shop, resting from their week long duties which had finished at lunchtime. No.68045 is standing on the Weigh House line and the entrance to that particular facility can be seen with a group of enthusiasts entering. The other J94 is stood on the Steaming Shed road. In the left background is the Stripping shed. Locomotives could be found in all sorts of nooks and crannies at this workshop - a superb place to visit in the days of steam. *BLP - DB406.*

Ex works after a General repair at Darlington (its last) L1 No.67757 resides on Darlington shed 30th June 1957, during its running in period. The King's Cross based engine did in fact require further works attention and returned to the shops the very next day for a couple of days 'fine tuning'. Except for a six month stay at Neasden shed in 1949, this L1 spent all of its short life allocated to depots on the East Coast Main Line - Hornsey, King's Cross and Grantham. The engine would return home via various jobs which would take it south over a couple of days. It may have worked some empty stock part of the way, piloted a passenger train or simply worked light engine for all or some of the journey. Its last visit to Darlington took place in August 1962 when on the third day of that month it entered the works for cutting up - not quite fourteen years old. *BLP - DB407.*

Standing just outside the main shed at Darlington motive power depot on the same June day in 1957 when 67757 was about the place, was another ex works six-coupled tank engine. V1 No.67648 looks resplendent with a new coat of black paint, complete with full lining and the new British Railways emblem. The Parkhead based engine looks ready to return home which in the circumstances was more than due because it had already had two false starts prior to this date. The V1 had arrived at Darlington Works on 13th May for a Light Intermediate repair which took a longer than normal amount of time but it was obviously having that new livery applied which explains the delay somewhat. However, it left the shops on 8th June for running-in, only to return to works on the 11th. By the 13th the problem was solved, or so it seemed. On the 21st it went back into the works for another Non-Classified repair and came out four days later. We see it now ready to work back to Glasgow for another couple of years employment on the Clydeside suburban services. At its next and penultimate visit to Darlington Works, in October 1959, it was converted to Class V3 which, with hindsight, seemed to be a senseless expense because over the two years following that rebuild it was never in regular service having first been ousted from its usual duties by electrification and then passed around from shed to shed trying to find suitable work. It returned to Darlington one more time, in February 1963 for scrapping. Prior to that it was laid up for more than a year at various dumps in Scotland. *BLP - DB409.*

The motive power depot at Darlington Bank Top underwent a near complete refurbishment during 1939-40. A new through running shed was built with adjacent repair shop, a mechanical coaling plant provided, 70ft turntable, a more efficient yard layout and a new office block, the latter seen here in the shape of a 1930's style 'semi'. The 1865 built roundhouse, with a 45ft diameter turntable, was retained, ideal for the numerous 0-6-0 tank engines on the depot's books. In June 1957 J72 No.69022 stands outside the 'semi' whilst its crew sit on bench seats taking in the afternoon sunshine - such was the rigors of shed pilot work on certain days. Although of pre-Group design, the J72 was younger than its surroundings having been built at Darlington in April 1951 - it was in fact younger than the first ten BR Standard's to be built. From the start it was allocated to Darlington shed doing much the same as seen here. On Sunday 10th September 1961 it transferred to West Hartlepool shed but was hard pressed to find any demanding work there. Condemned on the last day of 1962, it managed during its short lifetime to attend two General overhauls, one at Gateshead Works in April 1956 and the other at Darlington in March 1959. It used three different boilers over the eleven year period and finally entered Darlington Works on Tuesday 21st May 1963 for breaking up. *BLP - DB410.*

J21 No.65064, Darlington shed, June 1957. One of the depot's oldest inhabitants, this particular 0-6-0 started life at Gateshead Works in October 1890. By Grouping it was resident at West Hartlepool but in October 1935 it moved over to the west side of County Durham for a near twenty year convalescence of peace and tranquillity (well nearly) at the tiny one road shed situated alongside the river and the single platform passenger terminus at picturesque Wearhead. Its daily duty there saw it take the morning train to Darlington and return in the afternoon - job done. A 45ft turntable completed the facilities and coaling was taken care of at Darlington shed. For the record, the branch to Wearhead opened five years after this engine was built and closed in 1953. West Auckland was the next stop for this fortunate locomotive but not for long as Northallerton shed beckoned at the end of November 1954. That residency was short-lived also and Darlington acquired the engine in March 1955. In this view at the north end of the shed yard, the 0-6-0 appears ready for another branch job but that was probably not the case. More than likely it was now being used to haul 'dead' locomotives to and from the nearby works. After almost sixty-eight years of operational life the J21 entered Darlington Works for the last time on 9th September 1958 and was condemned six days later. *BLP - DB408.*

14

A5 No.69842 was one of the Hawthorn Leslie built members of the class which came into traffic in March 1926. For most of its life it was shedded to various depots in the north-east of England but in February 1951 it ventured south, really south, ending up at Norwich on the 25th of that month. A few weeks later it moved to Neasden then four weeks after that it went to Stratford. After just one month there it was back to Neasden, a shed which was at least familiar with the type. Obviously homesick the large tank returned north in July of that same year and resided at Darlington shed until June 1954 when Stockton required its services. With expanding diesel multiple unit services all over the former hunting grounds of this class, the inevitable withdrawals started. No.69842's turn came in October 1958 after more than a year in store at Saltburn. Seen here at Darlington Works in May 1959, the Pacific tank is still intact but not for long. Its 30-year expected lifespan is expired, its only value now is as scrap metal. *BLP - DB1557.*

This is the only 'Streak' in the book so treat it gently. A seemingly dead A4, No.60004 WILLIAM WHITELAW, is being marshalled around Darlington shed yard in late June 1965 by a green liveried Drewry 0-6-0 diesel mechanical shunter. By now based at Ferryhill shed in Aberdeen, the Pacific has come to the only workshop performing A4 repairs on BR. A few days after this photograph was captured on film the engine entered Darlington Works and over the next seven weeks received a Casual Light repair. Coming out on 28th August, the locomotive was good for another year working the 3-hour expresses between Aberdeen and Glasgow. The first four years of its life from new were spent working from King's Cross, Gateshead or Heaton sheds but in July 1941, after being renamed from the original GREAT SNIPE, it was transferred to Haymarket depot and for the next quarter of a century, until condemnation, it worked from just two Scottish sheds - Haymarket and Ferryhill. Withdrawn 17th July 1966, No.60004 appears to have done well compared with most others in the class, however, its demise saw it sold for scrap in October 1966 to a merchant in Wishaw. *BLP - DB7430.*

63361 resides inside the repair shop at Darlington shed in June 1965. Note the Heath Robinsonesque heating stove behind the oxy-acetylene set. The low level lockers are a reminder of the days when shed fitters had their own tools to carry out their trade. The dusty Q6 was in fact condemned and had come here from West Hartlepool, its home shed, earlier in the month to see if the Darlington shed fitters could fix it. Alas, this was the time on BR when anything other than simple repairs got a steam locomotive condemned. Within a few weeks No.63361 would be hauled away to the Ellis Metals scrapyard at Swalwell to join the list of twenty-seven other former BR locomotives which entered the yard intact and left in small pieces to feed the blast furnaces of Teesside. *BLP - DB7432.*

Situated between Gateshead and Pelaw, Felling station consisted an island platform to serve both Up and Down passenger lines, with separate goods lines kept away from the platform. Opened in 1896, Felling was similar to Pelaw in design with a central block of platform building surrounded by a canopy and accessed from the public highway by an inclined footway. Nowadays Felling is served by the Tyne & Wear Metro system, its main line status long gone but the freight lines are still in situ and operational. In June 1965 the station appears to be tidy but deserted as Tyne Dock bound Q6 No.63371 passes through. Note the paint job on the engine which has echoes of the 'official' photographs usually taken when steam locomotives were new. Even the lamp brackets have benefited from the painting applied to certain areas of the front end - its a shame the rest of the locomotive was not cleaned at the same time. Still with less than six months before oblivion, the dirt did not matter. Besides, three cheers for the staff at 52H for trying to brighten up their locomotive fleet in circumstances and conditions which would hardly lift anyone's morale. *BLP - DB7467.*

Having just been condemned, Peppercorn A1 No.60127 with its WILSON WORDSELL nameplates now removed, stands in the open at Gateshead engine shed, or what remained of the shed in June 1965. By this time the premier Tyneside depot was undergoing a complete refurbishment and the roundhouses which once stabled numerous LNER Pacifics were either demolished or had been altered into a straight road diesel depot where named Deltics now ruled the roost. In the background can be seen remnants of the former steam shed perched high on the south bank of the Tyne facing Newcastle city centre. The Pacific had spent its last eight months of operational life at 52A having transferred from Tweedmouth shed. It went north again in July 1965 but this time to Blyth where it was scrapped. *BLP - DB7518.*

Back in May 1959 Gateshead engine shed was pretty much intact with an allocation of A4, A3, A2 and A1 Pacifics. One of the less glamorous engines residing there was N10 No.69109 which had been allocated to the depot since it was built at Darlington in April 1903. A member of one of the smaller NER classes, No.69109 spent most of its life shunting at both goods and carriage sidings, for the latter job it had been fitted with a vacuum ejector in August 1930 at the adjacent Gateshead Works. Prior to that it was equipped with a Westinghouse brake only. At a General repair undertaken at Darlington Works, during September and October 1944, the vacuum brake and Westinghouse equipment was removed to be replaced by a steam brake. This restricted the engine to shunting goods wagons or banking and most of the class ended up in this condition, although a couple of the twenty engines either kept the vacuum ejector or had it refitted later for carriage shunting duties. Withdrawn on the 9th April 1962, No.69109 was one of the last three N10's. It was towed to Darlington for scrapping in June 1962 along with the other two N10, Nos.69097 from Bowes Bridge (a sub of Gateshead) and 69101 of Gateshead. *BLP - DB1526.*

The steam motive power depot at Heaton closed officially on 17th June 1963 but was afterwards used for the maintenance and storage of locomotives. It became something of a annex to Gateshead shed, which was undergoing tremendous alteration to fashion a diesel depot from the six square roundhouses and various small straight road sheds which made up that depot. In May 1964 Heaton housed a number of A3 Pacifics and a couple of V2's, besides a couple of English Electric Type 4 diesel locomotives. In this view a cold A3 No.60091 CAPTAIN CUTTLE, with a V2 behind, shelters inside the shed. Also on the premises were A3's Nos.60040 CAMERONIAN, 60051 BLINK BONNY, in steam whilst on rail tour duties and spruced up for the occasion, 60080 DICK TURPIN, and a named B1 No.61237 GEOFFREY H KITSON from Tyne Dock. All the A3's were allocated to Gateshead shed and all had been fitted with the Witte type smoke deflectors. The end was getting near for them but in the meantime they were being looked after and could be called upon to take up the reins within hours. Note that the shed has continuous smoke troughs over each road, a provision fitted by British Railways when they had the shed re-roofed in the early 1950's. *BLP - DB6745.*

In its last year of existence and working for a change, D49 No.62765 THE GOATHLAND waits to back onto a train at Hull (Paragon) station in August 1960. By now relegated to working secondary passenger and parcels trains, if such work could be found, these powerful Gresley 4-4-0s were regarded as time expired by 1960. Withdrawals started in 1957 with inroads made into the class during each year thereafter until the summer 1961 when the last examples were condemned. One of the 'Hunts', No.62768 THE MORPETH, had been withdrawn on 3rd November 1952 after receiving accident damage deemed too expensive to repair. Note the 4200, flush-sided Group Standard tender coupled to No.62765. This tender had started life coupled to D49 No.353 THE DERWENT (later 62761) on 12th September 1934. Renumbered to T7039 on 9th February 1939, the tender stayed with engine No.353 through to that engine's condemnation on 6th December 1957. After a period of storage at Darlington Works it was given to No.62765 from 16th May 1958 until that engine's withdrawal on 16th January 1961 when tender T7039 was also condemned and broken up. *BLP - DB5152.*

(opposite) **One of** Don Beecroft's earliest visits to the North Eastern Region was in September 1955 when he ventured over to Hull and called in at Dairycoates shed. Two of the residents he managed to get on film in the gloom of the shed were J72 No.68751 and, just in frame, N10 No.69107. This latter engine had been resident at 53A since 18th September 1949 after transfer from Gateshead. The 0-6-2T was no stranger to the Hull depot having spent its formative years there until 10th April 1937 when it moved to Tyneside. By now the N10 had finished all of its works visits, its last major overhaul being a 'General' at Gateshead Works in July 1954 when it also had a boiler change; the next call would be to Darlington in December 1957 for scrapping. The J72 was somewhat younger by twenty-two years, and was one of the ten built at Doncaster Works in late 1925. However, the 0-6-0T did not enjoy as long a life as No.69107, being condemned in May 1959, which was quite early for this large class especially so when compared with all the 19th Century Darlington built engines which outlived it by many months and in most cases by a number of years. The two engines are stabled in one of the two 1876 built roundhouses which stood at the eastern end of the shed complex, adjacent to the pedestrian entrance to the depot. It was in the year after this photograph was taken when the shed was re-roofed by BR in a massive rebuilding scheme which saw five of the depot's six roundhouses and the two straight road sheds rebuilt. The sixth roundhouse, and incidentally the last built in 1915, was demolished although its 60ft turntable and the radiating stabling roads were retained and continued to be used until about 1963 when the pits were filled in and the turntable lifted out. The whole depot closed in 1970 but some of the roundhouses remained standing and were later put to various industrial uses. Note the pieces of rope tied to the boiler handrails on both engines. These were used to secure the footplatemen's own bicycles which were taken with them so that when the crew were relieved at the end of shift in some local yard away from the shed, they could cycle home. The age old practice was accepted by the railway authorities in Hull District as a way of life. Its seems that every railwayman in Hull had a push bike then. *BLP - DB175.*

Gresley V3 No.67682 shunts the empty stock of a King's Cross train outside Hull (Paragon) in August 1960. By now allocated to Dairycoates engine shed because of the rebuilding of Botanic Gardens into a diesel depot, the 2-6-2T had only been in Hull since January 1959, ex Hexham shed. The class as a whole, including the earlier V1 engines had only been associated with the city since 1956 when five of them went to Botanic Gardens. When transfer to Dairycoates took place in June 1959, eight V1/V3's were involved. During the 1950's Dairycoates provided various engines for about thirty-two of the shunting and pilot turns in Hull District; Alexandra Dock supplied another seventeen whilst Botanic Gardens had five turns including an evening yard shunt at Goole prior to working a goods train back to Hull. Springhead shed had just three shunting turns for its engines, all in the local yard and environs. Shunting Paragon station and its carriage yard had originally been a Botanic job but when steam was expelled from that shed Dairycoates inherited the remaining shunting and pilot turns on which N.67682 is seen working. No.67682 was not one of those which was condemned in Hull, instead it went to Darlington at the end of November 1961 and worked from there until 23rd September 1963 when, with a life mileage of 721,703 behind it, it was withdrawn. Doncaster built in September 1939, it was Darlington scrapped in November 1963. Note the correct style of BR emblem, with the lion facing left, on the tank side. *BLP - DB5154.*

NEVILLE HILL

A3 No.60074 HARVESTER outside Neville Hill shed in May 1963. The photograph was taken shortly before its final journey, which took place on Tuesday 28th May, to Doncaster for cutting up. Withdrawn on the 8th April, this early rebuild from A1 class had been at the Leeds depot since December 1950 and had spent much of that time working to Newcastle with expresses from Leeds, Manchester and Liverpool. Finally ousted from that job by Type 4 diesel electric locomotives, which incidentally worked through from Lancashire all the way to Newcastle without any engine changing, the Pacific was actually due a General repair and boiler change in early 1963 so its time had run out. Note that the nameplates are still in situ - Doncaster would take care of those pieces of brass. Also, the Witte type smoke deflectors have not been fitted at a time when all the other surviving A3's were having them put on by necessity. Since its rebuilding in April 1928, No.60074 had in fact never been allocated to a depot south of Neville Hill, its services being shared by Gateshead, Haymarket, Heaton, York and of course the Leeds shed. The depot itself had recently undergone a massive facelift and two of the original four square type roundhouses had been demolished, the remaining two were given new roofs and new gable walls. The result is partly visible in this view. Later, when steam locomotives had been ousted from the shed, the turntables were removed and straight roads were laid in to accommodate the diesel locomotives and multiple units. *BLP - DB6146.*

Condemned and tenderless, A3 No.60081 SHOTOVER was another of the redundant Neville Hill Pacifics. Seen inside the shed in May 1963, No.60081 was about to be hauled out from its winter storage and got ready for the journey to Doncaster Works in the company of No.60074. Clustered around the Pacific are J39 No.64857 and a couple of exLMS 2-6-2 tank engines, with No.40048 on the same road as the A3 where the borrowed tender should be. Note that the chimney is still well covered even though the locomotive had been withdrawn some eight months previously when a General repair and boiler change was required but alas not authorised. This A3 was the one chosen by the LNER to carry the A.C.F.I. feed water heater which was fitted at Darlington Works during the summer of 1929. Not the most glamorous piece of equipment, nor cheap, it was somewhat complicated to the untrained and was both laborious and expensive to maintain. The French equipment was removed in February 1939. On a more positive note, this engine can be credited in having hauled the first non-stop *FLYING SCOTSMAN* in the Up direction - 1st May 1928. At the time it was allocated to Heaton shed and had recently been rebuilt from A1 class. No.60081 managed to spend the whole of its life allocated to engine sheds placed geographically within the boundaries of the former North Eastern Railway - Gateshead, Heaton, York and Neville Hill. *BLP - DB6147.*

In the days before the new locomotive depot was opened at Thornaby in June 1958, Newport engine shed housed a great variety of freight locomotives. Numerous WD 'Austerity' 2-8-0s rubbed shoulders with no less than forty-four Q6 0-8-0s when BR came into being. A similar number of 0-6-0 tender engines represented by classes J26 and J27 were also on the books at this time. However, the number of tank engines was low by comparison, with less than twenty in total and of those nearly half that number was accounted for by seven of the massive 4-8-0T of LNER Class T1. In July 1954 Newport shed could boast to housing eight of the by now thirteen strong class (nearby Stockton also had three) and one of those, No.69913, is seen having a weekend slumber with three WD 2-8-0s for company. By the middle of the decade the T1's began to disperse to other depots in the Region as newly delivered diesel shunters started to take on their duties in the Teesside yards. Besides, the new marshalling yard at Thornaby, simply named Tees Yard, would not require their services. No.69913 moved on to York at the end of October 1956 but was less than welcome there and its demise was confirmed a year later in December 1957 when it was condemned at Darlington Works. One of the original ten Gateshead built members of the class, No.69913 had spent virtually all its working life at Newport since being put into traffic in November 1909. Such was the usefulness of the class at Grouping, it was decided to construct another five, this time at Darlington and it was one of these 1925 vintage engines which became the last T1 in service, bowing out in June 1961, Tyne Dock based No.69921 had survived the penultimate withdrawals of the class by more than eighteen months. The two 1890-built roundhouses at Newport depot, along with the three road straight shed put up by the LNER during WW2, were vacated on 1st June 1958 when the allocation moved to the new depot at Thornaby. Demolition soon followed and the site was used for further sidings in connection with the new Tees Yard. *BLP - DB5175.*

CAMBOIS

A trip to the north-east was not complete in the days of steam without a visit to one of the NCB railway systems which appeared to be virtually everywhere in County Durham and Northumberland. In June 1965 National Coal Board 0-6-0ST No.18 is seen passing the British Railways signal box at Cambois with a train of empty wagons. The NCB kept steam motive power going for many years after BR had banished it and during the 1970's many rail enthusiasts would venture to one or more of the various Coal Board systems in this part of England purely to get a 'fix' of proper working steam. Alas even that privilege has now gone forever, along with the numerous coal mines the lines served. The level crossing here was gated for both the NCB line and the two BR tracks. These two routes ran independently but parallel to each other from Cambois Colliery to staiths at North Blyth, following the coastline and sand dunes all the way. Just by the BR engine shed at North Blyth there was a connection from the shed yard to the NCB line. At North Blyth the NCB had its own separate installation from the BR facility, nearer to the mouth of the River Blyth. That would be from where this train was returning from. *BLP - DB7448.*

On BR trackage, J27 No.65794 has a loaded train of coal at Cambois in early June 1965. The load of ubiquitous coal hoppers was en route to the BR staiths at North Blyth and would not have been too taxing for this 0-6-0 over a fairly easy route where a leisurely pace was the norm. A number of collieries in the area sent coal to the North Blyth staiths and the ex NER engine shed at that place provided most of the motive power. No.65794 was one of the North Blyth complement and had been so since November 1950 when it transferred from nearby Percy Main. Shortly after this working the J27 was condemned and later sold for scrap, just a year short of its 60th birthday. *BLP - DB7452.*

North Blyth engine shed was within sight of South Blyth engine shed but the stretch of water that separated the two establishments required a journey of several rail miles if any engine was transferred. North Blyth was the dominant depot with the South shed as its sub although both had similar allocations. The depot on the north shore was a square roundhouse design, much favoured by the North Eastern Railway in the latter period of shed building. Opened in 1896, it was amongst the last of the steam sheds on the North Eastern Region and was closed in September 1967, the sub having closed some months before in May. Peppercorn K1 No.62022 was typical of the motive power using North Blyth as home, ex LMS Ivatt moguls, with funny numbers beginning with 4, were also here at the end and these engines had actually been allocated to 52F longer than these Peppercorn moguls. The other type to be found here was the former NER 0-6-0 of LNER Class J27 although by June 1965, when this scene was captured, their numbers were dwindling fast. Note the former gunpowder van which was now part of the depot's breakdown train. *BLP - DB7504.*

J27 No.65812, seen outside its new home at South Blyth shed June 1965, shortly before setting out for a local colliery to begin trip working coal hoppers to the staiths. This 0-6-0 was an orphan from Percy Main shed which had closed to steam during the previous February. To date, the engine had spent most of its life from new at the latter shed although during that near fifty-seven years, from May 1908 to February 1965, it had actually spent two years working at the former Great Eastern shed at Peterborough East. That interlude had taken place from 15th December 1926 to 2nd January 1929 after which the 0-6-0 never left exNER territory again. The engines' foray to former GE lines was not unaccompanied and four other saturated members of the class joined it at Peterborough, 'on loan' and all returned by 1929. Besides these five J27's, twelve superheated engines also took flight to exGE lines on a more permanent basis with Cambridge and March sheds sharing them equally at first later on New England had some but at the outbreak of war they slowly made their way back home via Retford, Ardsley and a few other unfamiliar depots. Up to its closure, Percy Main shed always had a large proportion of this 115 strong class allocated, rarely did the number drop below twenty. It was only towards the end of steam on BR that the class began to allocate to the two Blyth depots and at the end of NE Region steam workings, in September 1967, the survivors of the class congregated at either North Blyth and Sunderland sheds, a fitting end to their lifetime of hauling coal. No.65812 nearly got to be amongst the elite which saw the end but fate got in the way. It was booked down to reallocate to Sunderland shed two days before the closure of South Blyth but some mechanical problem must have surfaced and the engine was stopped. Still at South Blyth shed on 5th June 1967, it was condemned and sold in August to local scrap merchant Hughes Bolckow. *BLP - DB7456.*

J27 No.65855 inside the four road shed at South Blyth June 1965. Note the smoke vents are once again individual units rather than one continuous trough along each road. The smoke haze is evident but the ventilation was adequate enough for photography. This engine was one of the Beyer, Peacock batch built at the same time as No.65812 which came from North British Locomotive Co. No.65855 spent all of its life in NER territory, starting life at Newport, moving to Stockton for a couple of years in 1935, then Haverton Hill until Thornaby called in February 1959. South Blyth took receipt on 6th January 1963, during one of the coldest winters of modern times. This J27 was one of the lucky ones and transferred to Sunderland on the day that South Blyth officially closed, 28th May 1967. It was still in working order when the end came at Sunderland - all the fires were dropped and everything was condemned. Within a few weeks the cold, silent 0-6-0 was hauled away to a scrapyard in Stockton to join the throng of thousands that had already been broken up or were soon to be. *BLP - DB7459*.

The coaling 'plant' at South Blyth engine shed was a typical North Eastern manual coaling stage with ramped access for the wagons, substantial timber beams forming a bufferstop, coal spouts and dilapidated cladding around a semi-open coaling shed. Beneath the coaling stage were 'facilities' for the staff with a Cleaners' mess room, a lavatory and a brick store. Now doubt the coalmen used the same mess room as the engine cleaners but by 1966 the latter group would have been virtually non-existent. Resident J27 No.65819 is having its tender topped up with both coal and water at the same time in this September 1966 view, the North Eastern Railway being amongst the minority in providing water columns at the faces of their coaling stages. The 0-6-0 is virtually ready for another round of colliery trip working. When closure of the depot to steam locomotives took place in May 1967, diesel motive power used the shed until the following January when they too were evicted. However, the diesels had a new depot to call home at Cambois albeit some distance to the north of this facility. *BLP - DB8309.*

During the last full year of steam working on the North Eastern Region, full use was made of the available locomotives, mostly J27 0-6-0s, K1 2-6-0s, Q6 0-8-0s, WD 2-8-0s and the exLMS Ivatt 2-6-0s. Here at the closed North Seaton station in September 1966, one of the latter type, No.43000 (wearing a 12A Carlisle Kingmoor shed plate) is heading south with a mineral train from one of the Ashington group of coal mines. Note the shunting pole lay across the running plate below the smokebox, a sure sign of NER practice. This section of railway was opened in two stages some thirteen years apart. The line from the junction at Bedlington northwards to North Seaton dated from 1859 and the ongoing route from North Seaton to Ashington and Newbiggin opened in 1872. The station here closed to passengers in November 1964 just a year later than the goods facilities closed. However, coal traffic continued to used the line as long as the collieries were open. Note the passenger facilities on this platform do not reflect the elaborate buildings on the opposite platform - no matter, the station and all its associated buildings was demolished by 1972. In the year before its closure the station apparently had only three regular daily passengers and was obviously a prime candidate for the Beeching axe. *BLP - DB8311.*

Just east of Gateshead was Pelaw which was the divergence of three routes. The most northerly went to South Shields via Jarrow and Tyne Dock. The middle route, in an easterly direction, went ultimately to Sunderland but offered alternatives to Tyne Dock and the collieries on the south bank of the Tyne. The final route struck out in a southerly direction towards Teesside via Washington and Penshaw. Q6 No.63455 of Tyne Dock shed is approaching from the latter route in September 1966 with a loaded westbound coal train. This 0-8-0 was a late arrival at Tyne Dock shed, going there in May 1965 after spending twenty-two years at Consett depot. Nearly forty-seven years old when withdrawn on 22nd June 1967, it ended up at a scrapyard in Chesterfield during the following August. *BLP - DB8324.*

39

Traversing the same track through Pelaw a few hours later, an unidentified 350 h.p. 0-6-0 diesel shunter has Peppercorn K1 No.62007 in tow. At first glance it appears that a dead steam locomotive is en route to either main works for repair or worse still, a scrapyard. However, the K1 was in fact allocated to Sunderland shed when this scene was being enacted in September 1966 and it was later transferred to Tyne Dock shed on 23rd October 1966. So what is the story behind this picture? Perhaps the K1 was being moved prematurely to Tyne Dock shed but why come via Pelaw with a reversal being required when the more direct route from Sunderland would have taken it via East Boldon and the junction just west of that place. Perhaps the engine had failed somewhere in the locality and was being taken to Gateshead shed for attention. What appear to be boiler tubes are lay on the running plate with some rope for security. Its one of those nice mystery photographs which require an answer. So dear reader, if you have any idea why No.62007 was passing through Pelaw in this fashion in September 1966 then the Publisher would like to know. Perhaps the answer, if one surfaces, might appear in another of the titles in this ongoing series. *BLP - DB8327.*

The constant movement of coal and its derivatives along the lines radiating out from the great rivers of north-east England - the Tyne, Wear and Tees, not to mention the coastal ports too - was, for nearly 150 years, the sole reason for the North Eastern Railway having a steam locomotive fleet dominated by goods tender engines. More than seven hundred and fifty 0-6-0 tender engines, spread over eight main classes (J21-J28), managed the bulk of the work throughout the LNER era. They were helped out by a few hundred 0-8-0 tender engines which took on some of the heavier work and the longer distance jobs. Of course as one particular class wore out they were replaced by other newer designs, or so it appears in theory. On the North Eastern Region at the very end of steam haulage, some of the pre-Grouping types were still going strong as witness J27 No.65879 at Percy Main in July 1965 with a train of well loaded coal hoppers. Shedded at North Blyth at the time of the photograph, the 0-6-0 moved to South Blyth in October 1966 then, in a move which would ensure its place in history, it was transferred to Sunderland from where it worked until condemned aged forty-five years, on 9th September 1967, and was amongst the last of NE steam. The NE Region was a big user of the hopper wagon for coal movement and the origins of this type of wagon can be traced way back to virtually the beginning of main line railways in this country when the constituent companies of the North Eastern Railway and the colliery owners who managed their own wagon fleets, decided on a wagon design which would easily unload at the coal staithes on the riverside and dock facilities. Thus the bottom discharge wagon was born and is still preferred today where rapid easy discharge of the load can speed up the usage of wagons to the point of requiring a lot less of them. Elsewhere in England, Scotland and Wales, the square, flat bottom, wooden (later steel) sided mineral wagon was sufficient where wagons were unloaded manually in coal merchants yards or were either tipped end on or completely over at specialist facilities. A train of hopper wagons as depicted here was also colourful with various shades of grey going into dark maroon via yellow rust and brown rust. However, most of us did not take too much notice of the wagon stock of the trains which passed by then, the motive power was what mattered. *BLP-DB7536.*

41

Don Beecroft appears to have made only one visit to Scarborough when he used his camera - no matter because the pictures he recorded are safely archived. We start the selection with D49 No.62739 THE BADSWORTH, which was the pilot at Scarborough (Landsdowne Road) station on a superb sunny day in July 1960. This was another D49 working out its last days on any duty it was allowed to perform. When it travelled to Darlington Works in October 1960, it was in need of a boiler change but at that time in the lives of the D49's it was more likely to be condemned and, after an examination on the 11th, the 4-4-0 was duly withdrawn and cut up shortly afterwards. Allocated to Scarborough shed since 1st July 1951, the authorities at Scarborough must have had high hopes when this engine arrived from Neville Hill and was promptly dispatched to Darlington Works for a 'General'. Every two years thereafter the engine received a heavy repair to keep it in good condition for the somewhat light work it undertook from Scarborough shed. Nice view of the signal gantry. *BLP - DB4063*.

By the summer of 1960 the allocation of Scarborough engine shed was 'a little thin on the ground'. The last pre-Grouping design on the books, in the shape of A8 No.69885 was condemned on the 20th June. LNER designed engines consisted of two D49's, No.62739 and No.62762 THE FERNIE, both condemned in October. Recently allocated D49's which had gone for scrap in the previous couple of years were No.62756 in April 1958, Nos.62735 and 62769 in August and September respectively of the same year, Nos.62745 and 62751 in Match 1959. No.62770 escaped to Selby in June 1959 but was condemned three months later at York. Two J72's had come and gone, No.68739 for scrap in August 1959 with No.69016 leaving for York in December 1958. Two ex LMS Cl.4 2-6-4Ts, Nos.42084 and 42085 had left for Whitby in June 1958. From the same company 0-6-0T No.47403 was still allocated to Scarborough in July 1960 and would be until it went for scrap in September of the following year. British Railways Standard designs were the latest newcomers and departures with four Class 5's, Nos.73167, 73168, 73169 and 73170 leaving the depot for greener pastures in June 1959. for the record the first went to Normanton whilst the other three transferred to Holbeck. Another resident was BR Std. Cl.3 No.77004 which hung around until April 1963 when the shed was effectively closed. That 2-6-0 was joined by No.77013 in October 1960 and both engines went to York shed. The final BR Standard design calling Scarborough home in July 1960 were the four Cl.3 2-6-2 tank engines numbered 82026 to 82029, which had come from Low Moor and Malton sheds, the first two arriving in September 1958 and the other pair in June 1960. No.82026 is about to take on some water at Landsdowne Road in July 1960 against a background of Metro-Camm diesel multiple units. All four of the Cl.3 tanks had left Scarborough before the shed closed - all went on to further employment. *BLP - DB4067.*

43

The D49 pilot goes about its mundane duties in July 1960. Note coach set No.157 of which the leading vehicle is Brake Third E80038E. *BLP - DB4070.*

(opposite) **Departure time at Scarborough and B16/3 No.61418, of York shed, leaves Landsdown Road station in grand style with a Leeds bound excursion, the first two vehicles of which appear to be exLMS designs. The curling exhaust from the chimney manages to cast a giant shadow over both engine and train on this beautiful July evening; only the adjacent d.m.u. mars an otherwise excellent setting but it was the age of massive transition on BR. The 4-6-0 had spent most of its life working in Yorkshire after arriving at Dairycoates from Tyne Dock shed in December 1936. In June 1940 it was based at York, to be joined there by the rest of the class in 1943 under a wartime concentration scheme. As No.922, its first LNER number, it spent a whole twelve months of those wartime years, from 7th April 1943 to 1st April 1944, incarcerated inside Darlington Works awaiting parts for its rebuilding to a Part 3 engine. After twenty-two years away from Dairycoates shed, it returned to Hull in December 1962 and was withdrawn from there in June 1964. During the following October it was cut up at Albert Draper's scrapyard in Hull.** *BLP - DB4069.*

Dairycoates K3 No.61922 backs down to couple onto coach set No.157. This engine was one of the Armstrong Whitworth built examples of the class and entered traffic in August 1934 and Heaton shed. After a couple of months on Tyneside it moved north to Tweedmouth where it settled in for a four and a half year stint working north and south of the border. Back to Heaton in March 1939, it worked throughout the war from either Gateshead or Heaton sheds. Hull Dairycoates gained the K3 in May 1946, a welcome addition to the allocation. Its last major repair, a 'General', took place just six months before this photograph was taken but the dirt and grime accumulated during that period has built up so much that lining and numbers are becoming difficult to discern. By the time it went to Doncaster Works for the last time, and ultimately oblivion in May 1962, it must have worn a thick coat of grime. Cleaners at Dairycoates had been in short supply for years. The destination of the train will be Leeds. *BLP - DB4074.*

(opposite) Another evening departure, this one with B1 No.61229 in charge of a Bradford excursion. The magnificent signal gantry has been partially obscured but we can forgive the B1 which is putting up another fine exhaust. The Hammerton Street based 4-6-0 has a fine mixture of coaching stock in tow which, on return to Bradford, would spend the rest of the week stabled in one of the carriage sidings of which every large town in Britain use to have dotted all over the local network. The coaches would come out for the following weekend or Bank Holiday excursions and do so until the end of the season - Blackpool Illuminations extended the season into October for many. Then, the stock was put away for the winter, only to come out for the Easter specials and excursions and so it went on, year in, year out. What happened to all that stock and the yards they lived in - like much of the steam age railway infrastructure on mainland UK - its gone forever. Thank goodness for memory and photographs. *BLP - DB4073.*

The K3 gets underway as the sun sinks lower in the west. Other excursions departing after this train, when the sun was sinking so fast that photography became impossible, included one heading for Doncaster with B1 No.61131, a King's Cross excursion (351) with V2 No.60867 in charge, and a Burton-on-Trent bound train with ex LMS 'Crab' No.42922 as motive power. *BLP - DB4079.*

STARBECK

Starbeck engine shed yard, June 1957, with Neville Hill Q6 No.63436 and New England V2 No.60897 being late afternoon visitors to the North Yorkshire depot. The shed's normal complement of motive power at this time could produce nothing larger than J39 class for freight traffic with D49's sufficing for the passenger work behind. Although plenty of heavy traffic between the West Riding and Teeside passed through Harrogate, the town did not generate anything like the amount of traffic to require eight coupled goods engines and six coupled passenger engines. The shed itself comprised a long two road building situated in the fork of lines created by the Harrogate-York and Harrogate-Leeds routes. Coaling was somewhat mechanically primitive with a coaling crane being employed, a coaling stage was never provided. The depot could boast a Breakdown train and one the ancient vans' making up that train can be seen behind the 0-8-0. *BLP - DB405.*

49

One of Manningham's Stanier Class 3 2-6-2Ts, No.40112, had worked into Harrogate from Bradford during June 1957, probably for the annual Harrogate Show. Other engines on shed included a couple of visiting WD 2-8-0s, albeit arriving on goods trains. *BLP - DB411.*

Being on the edge of LNER territory, Starbeck shed attracted locomotives from the former LMS lines nearby. However, this particular May 1959 visitor was actually allocated to Goole depot so could hardly be described as a visitor in the circumstances. In fact, this engine spent some fifteen years of its twenty-eight year life allocated to sheds which were in the North Eastern Region. The Stanier six-coupled tank, No.42477, had a somewhat interesting lifetime allocation history which started at Patricroft in January 1937. In April 1940 it moved to South Wales for a year at Swansea followed by three years at Stafford. In May 1944 it went up to Scotland for two years working from Polmadie. Then it was back to Manchester for four years at Newton Heath. In September 1950 it began its relationship with the NE Region by transferring to Goole (admitted not then part of the NER but soon to be, so it counts). Nearly six years later it moved westwards to Mirfield for a two year stint, then to York for three months in June 1958 before settling at Neville Hill for the pre-Christmas winter season. Goole shed got it back in January 1959 and in June it moved to York again, this time for a full year before going to Malton in June 1960. In December 1961 Darlington shed acquired the engine and kept hold of it until June 1965 when it was sent back to the LM Region at Chester. Alas, its services were no longer required at that place and withdrawal took place. A private scrapyard carried out the final act. *BLP - DB1502.*

Hiding in the background of the last illustration was J39 No.64944, seen now in all its glory outside Starbeck shed in May 1959. A long time resident, arriving in July 1940 from Selby, this 0-6-0 would survive the shed closure, which took place in September 1959, and move on to York. The length of the shed at Starbeck can be appreciated from this view of the south-easterly aspect, the two-road structure having undergone re-roofing during 1956. Long before that date the roof was virtually non-existent and it seems strange to spend so much money shortly before the place was due for closure when it was necessary more than fifteen years beforehand. BR were careful to fit smoke troughs for the whole length of the shed building, the parsimonious ways of the North Eastern Railway being swept aside in favour of the extravagant and somewhat belated expense laid out here. To finish off the scheme, the interior walls were even treated to a good 'splash' of whitewash. *BLP - DB1504.*

Three D49's, comprising two 'Hunts' and an 'ex-Shire', laid up at Starbeck shed in May 1959. Stored on a siding on the east side of the shed yard, alongside the coal stack, all three engines still had their name, number and shed plates in situ, a sign that they were in storage awaiting further employment rather than withdrawn and stored awaiting scrapping - by 1959 either reason could be the case. Nearest the camera is No.62759 THE CRAVEN, next is No.62763 THE FITZWILLIAM. Behind that was a Shire-cum-Hunt, with an ex-GC type stepped out tender, No.62727 THE QUORN (formerly BUCKINGHAMSHIRE). It was unusual to find these ex-GC tenders behind the D49 Part 2 engines but No.62727 had been coupled to this example (T5133) since August 1949. Anyway, the 'Hunts' still had a future of sorts in front of them and shortly after this scene was captured they were put back into traffic and worked through the summer prior to being transferred to Hull Dairycoates when Starbeck closed on the 13th September. At Dairycoates the work was sporadic to say the least and more time was spent in store than being out on the road. Both Dairycoates and the closed Hull & Barnsley shed at Springhead were used for storage during the latter months of the class. The 4-4-0s were hauled to Darlington Works in January 1961 and were condemned within days of each other. All of them were cut up shortly afterwards. Two other 'Hunts' on Starbeck shed that day were No.62738 THE ZETLAND and No.62765 THE GOATHLAND. The former also left Starbeck on the 13th September but went to York instead and after a week there it was condemned. No.62765 ended up at Dairycoates with the others but took a less direct journey leaving Starbeck in mid June on being transferred to Selby. *BLP - DB1503.*

SUNDERLAND SOUTH DOCK
ENGINE SHED

By May 1959 Sunderland South Dock engine shed was home to a large number of A8 4-6-2T engines. In this line-up we see Nos.69852, 69854 and 69873, all of which were still in employment at that time. Out of a class total of forty-five, there was only twenty-one A8's still extant at the end of 1959 and most of them were at Sunderland although No.69852 had succumbed on 4th November so did not count in that statistic. No.69854 lasted until May 1960 before it got the final call to Darlington. No.69873, a relative newcomer to South Dock shed having spent most of its allocated time there sub-shedded at Durham, was condemned in February 1960. This engine had started life as an A8 at Neville Hill but after a month it moved to Scarborough at the end of May 1935. In December of that year it transferred to Botanic Gardens shed in Hull for a thirteen year residency. In September 1948 Middlesbrough was its home for a couple of years before moving back to Hull for six months. Leaving Botanic Gardens for the last time in November 1950 it returned to Middlesbrough for a five year stay after which it was allocated to West Hartlepool in July 1955. Sunderland had it 'on the books' from 15th September 1957. The Sunderland based A8's which hung on to the end of the class in June 1960 were: 69850, 69870, 69878, 69883. *BLP - DB1513.*

Tyne Dock engine shed never had an allocation of Pacific tender engines and it is true to say that none were ever associated in any way with the place until the summer of 1965 when withdrawn Peppercorn A1's were stored there. This particular building was actually a wagon shop at one time but that activity had ceased some time prior to the next door engine shed taking over the four road building for locomotive repair and storage. Shorn of nameplates, numberplates, shedplates and worksplates, the magnificent express passenger engines lay idle and forlorn with no hope of ever working again. They were laid up awaiting a buyer - to be more precise a scrap merchant with yard space and a few grand to take away these leviathans of the steam age. The money side of the purchasing process was not a problem for most scrap yards, the problem seemed to be space because by 1965 BR had finished scrapping steam locomotives at its various works and was selling the thousands of redundant steam locomotives to private concerns. However, the private concerns were inundated with locomotives, their yards bulging at the seams. It was a feeding frenzy for the blast furnaces and a time to make some money for the merchants. These engines would soon find a buyer and within no time at all they would become but a memory. Some, like No.60142 here, still had a few tons of coal in their tenders which was hardly likely to be emptied before it was hauled away for scrap. Note the dreaded word chalked on the tender and cab sides. *BLP - DB7543.*

For the record there were five A1's at Tyne Dock on this July day in 1965 - 60116 HAL O'THE WYND; 60132 MARMION and 60142 EDWARD FLETCHER had all been condemned on 14th June 1965 and were ex Gateshead, having arrived at Tyne Dock shed en masse on 11th March 1965. The three engines were sold to Hughes Bolckow at Blyth in July and they were taken north during the month. The fourth and fifth engines, 60129 GUY MANNERING and 60151 MIDLOTHIAN were also ex Gateshead shed but had not yet been condemned, and were simply being stored. On 11th July the pair were given a reprimand, steamed and transferred to York shed from where they worked until 11th October in the case of 60129, and the end of November when 60151's time finally ran out. Both were later sold for scrap. No.60129 made the long journey to R.A.King's yard at Norwich in November, whilst 60151 went no furthe than Wath to meet it's end. *BLP - DB7544.*

The more usual fare to be found at Tyne Dock engine shed was represented by this BR Standard 9F 2-10-0 No.92061 in July 1965. Although looking grubby - weren't they all by now - this ten year old engine was one of the batch dedicated to the Consett iron ore train workings and was fitted with Westinghouse air pumps for the wagon door security devices. 92061 was one of seven 9F's (92060-92066) equipped with Westinghouse. All were delivered to Tyne Dock from Crewe Works during November and December 1955. In the following summer three more Westinghouse fitted engines, Nos.92097-92099, arrived new from Crewe. The 9F's would often work the 800-ton, nine wagon iron ore trains in pairs, one pulling and one pushing but they were singly capable of lifting the trains over the 22 miles of heavily graded route to the steel works at Consett. All of the late 1955 batch of 9F's, except one No.92065 which escaped to Wakefield in November 1966, were withdrawn from Tyne Dock shed, indeed the first of them to go, No.92066, was already subject to a purchase order for scrap when 92061 posed for this photograph. The three from 1956 were also withdrawn at Tyne Dock, all in 1966. Besides the Westinghouse 9F's, another member of the class was tried out on the iron-ore services - one of the ill-starred stoker-fitted engines No.92167. Arriving in May 1962 it was relegated to the banking role as it was not equipped with air pumps but it was sent packing back to Saltley in the following October after a less than glorious debut. The stoker was removed afterwards at Crewe Works. *BLP - DB7552.* 61

Tyne Dock engine shed required specialist engines for the Consett iron ore workings. Firstly the engines had to have enough power to haul the heavy trains from virtually sea level at Terminus Quay to the 900ft altitude of the steel works at Consett. Secondly, from 1951 onwards, the engines had to be equipped with two Westinghouse pumps to work in conjunction with the new large bogie hopper wagons introduced during that year. One pump kept the air operated doors closed whilst the other pump was used to open them whilst the train was still on the move over the unloading bins. Initially the first engines to be equipped were Q7 0-8-0s which had been working the trains for years when they had ordinary hopper wagons. The new wagons had a capacity of fifty-six tons and each train comprised eight wagons for one of these locomotives, nine for the 9F's. In September 1951 five Thompson O1 class 2-8-0s (63712, 63755, 63760, 63856 and 63874) were transferred to Tyne Dock and from April 1952 they too were each fitted with two 10-inch Westinghouse pumps at Gorton Works. To brake the iron ore trains a vacuum ejector had also to be put on each engine. O1 No.63712, seen at Tyne Dock shed in May 1959, was the first of the five equipped to work the new block trains. The five O1's were no strangers to the north-east, nor to Tyne Dock as some of them had been allocated to what became the NE Region since conversion from O4 to O1 in 1944. Working alongside the Q7's and later the 9F's, the O1's handled the traffic as required. All five were withdrawn together on 26th November 1962 and they gradually found their way back to Gorton for breaking up. *BLP - DB1535.*

Just finishing its duty, Q6 No.63389 makes its way home hauling a brakevan. Home was Tyne Dock shed, seen in the background of this July 1965 picture. The Q6 started its operational career at this depot in December 1917 and after a near twenty year absence working from Teesside sheds from 1943, it returned to Tyne Dock in December 1962. The month of December was to prove something of an omen for this engine because five months after this scene was captured No.63389 was condemned on the 27th December. Two months later it was sold for scrap and hauled away to Blyth. The future of Tyne Dock engine shed was no more secure than that of the 0-8-0. Although home to some of the largest freight locomotives on BR including members of the Thompson O1 class, Q7, WD 2-8-0 and the 9F 2-10-0, the depot facilities were hardly in keeping with its allocation. Admitted the covered accommodation was there but it consisted of three roundhouses and a small four road straight shed. Two of the roundhouses had turntables no bigger than 42ft diameter whilst the largest roundhouse had a turntable of only 50ft diameter - none of which were of any use to the eight and ten coupled engines just described. The LNER did, however, provide a 60ft turntable in front of the shed on the west side of the yard but that was all. The big boys basically had to 'rest' outside. *BLP - DB7564.*

63

D20 No.62388 was a fairly recent addition to the West Hartlepool shed allocation when it was seen on the shed yard in July 1952. The class had been associated with the shed since the 1930's with four or five of them handling the passenger, parcels and fitted freight services. Relegated from their previous duties on the main line, these 4-4-0s were trustworthy and extremely useful engines. The West Hartlepool batch would often work as far as Leeds via Northallerton and Harrogate. Originally the class consisted sixty engines, all built at Gateshead Works in batches of ten between 1899 and 1907. No.62388, as NER No.1210, fell into the last batch. Fifty of the class survived to become BR property and the last ones were not withdrawn until 1957. Although not in pristine condition, No.62388 nevertheless had a few more years work ahead of it and on leaving West Hartlepool for Northallerton shed in October 1952 it went on to Tyne Dock in January of the following year but returned to Northallerton in March to finish its days there. Withdrawal took place at the end of April 1954. *BLP - DB5161.*

J72 No.68722 shunts at Stranton Junction, West Hartlepool in May 1959. Working out its last months of life, this 0-6-0T was one of the longer-lived examples built for the North Eastern Railway in April 1922 by Armstrong Whitworth. Within four years of the Grouping the engine left Darlington shed and was sent to the southern extremes of the LNER. As No.2315 it was allocated to four different sheds in 1927 - Cambridge, Peterborough East, Immingham and Retford, in that order. During 1928 Gorton had its services then Ardsley and finally, back in more familiar territory, York. It resided at York for the next thirty years and for the last five of them, from August 1953, it was fitted with both a vacuum ejector and steam heating for working the York station pilot duty. Haverton Hill got it in late June 1958 but they had no use for it so sent it on to West Hartlepool. Hardly a great centre for passenger train stock marshalling, the mainly freight locomotive depot used it in the local yards until the diesel shunters arrived. In February 1960 it was sent to Darlington Works who promptly condemned it and then cut it up. In this view we see one of the shunting staff leaping from the locomotive steps ready for the next cut to be made whilst the ensemble was still on the move. Great days when even simple shunting operations were interesting to observe, and listen to. *BLP - DB1559.*

Whistling its way along, English Electric Type 4 D253 of York depot, treads an unfamiliar route through West Hartlepool with a diverted Newcastle-King's Cross express in June 1965. Approaching the crossing at Stranton Junction, the torturous course of the main line through Hartlepool is nearly behind it now, only the junction at Newburn to negotiate and then the big, noisy, 2000 horsepower engine can be opened up for a quick dash over to Stockton. The weeds and general unkempt appearance of the surrounding railway infrastructure can be compared with the previous view taken six years before. The run down of the railway in this part of the country during the last decade of steam working was both rapid and depressing and it is amazing that 'backwaters' such as Hartlepool managed to keep a line at all. Today, local industries and a reasonable passenger service keep the tracks shiny and occasionally main line diversions such as this take place to add a bit of variety but you won't see any 133 ton monsters like this any more - unless you are lucky. *BLP - DB7471.*

With less than six months of operational life ahead of it, Thompson A2/2 No.60504 MONS MEG departs from York with a morning Newcastle-King's Cross working in July 1960. This Pacific had been based at New England depot since transferring from Haymarket shed in January 1950. Unable to fully trust the unreliable Thompson A2 Part 2 class, the BR motive power authorities allocated them where they were not first choice for the heavy and fast express passenger workings for which they were originally intended to work. New England and York sheds were the ideal locations because they could act in a stand-by capacity for any failing A1, A3 and A4 locomotives which had principal charge of the ECML expresses. They could also be entrusted to work the less important express and secondary passenger workings on the main line along with parcels and fast goods trains. By the end of 1950, having been tried at all the main passenger depots on the ECML, the six engines which made up the class were split equally between New England and York, a situation which continued until their somewhat premature condemnations over the period from November 1959 to July 1961. *BLP - DB4060.*

K1 No.62060 brings a southbound fish train from Scarborough into York station on a warm evening in May 1964. This scene, from forty-odd years ago, was being enacted virtually hourly all over the Eastern and North Eastern Regions - not to mention the Scottish and London Midland Regions - and everyday dozens of fish trains were making their way from the east coast fishing ports to the hinterland markets. Hull alone could send out as many as fourteen fish trains each weekday but along with all the other fishing ports that rail traffic is now down to nil. The 1960's brought about many changes in rail traffic and it was not just fish traffic with declined, the movement of livestock was terminated along with the many commodities movements which were lost to road transport. This York based K1 fared no better and after moving to North Blyth in August 1966, chasing work, it moved again in march of the following year to Tyne Dock but it was laid up in the summer and withdrawn on 2nd August. By the end of September 1967 it was in the hands of Blyth scrap merchant Hughes, Bolckow. *BLP - DB6762.*